THANKS, AWFULLY!

A Comedy in One Act

By

JEAN LEE LATHAM

CHICAGO

THE DRAMATIC PUBLISHING COMPANY

Notice

PRINTED IN THE UNITED STATES OF AMERICA

(THANKS, AWFULLY!)

THANKS, AWFULLY!

Originally produced at the Williams School Little Theatre, February 10 and 11, 1928, with the following cast:

RICHARD MONTAGUE, *a woman hater*		Clarence Straight
DOROTHY MONTAGUE, *his sister*		Pauline Feinstein
MARION GATEWOOD, *"the girl"*		Judith E. Cohn
ANN MARSH, *Marion's friend*		Irma Cushman
CAROL	*Dorothy's friends*	Agnes Legg
EDITH		Thelma Hanley
MRS. DODD		Christine Tillotson
MRS. SMYTHE		Lemira Stratton
ENID		Elsie Waters
NANETTE		Pauline B. See
MRS. HEMINGWAY		Ernestine Brown
MRS. JAMES-GOWER		Esther Covert
CAROLINE		Barbara Witter
JANE		Edith Quackenbush

PLACE: *The living-room of the Montague apartment.*
TIME: *The present. Evening.*

THANKS, AWFULLY

SCENE: *The living-room of* DICK *and* DOT'S *apartment. Through French doors, center back, a room where the bridge tables are laid is visible. A fireplace is down right, with a long divan, backed with a slender table, pulled companionably before it. Back stage, at the extreme right, is a huge over-stuffed chair with a smoking stand close by. Back, left, is a grand piano, and down stage to the lower front corner of the piano, is another chair. A small console table with a mirror above it is down left. Two lamps, one at the upper end of the divan, and one between the piano and an easy chair, invite one to lounge and knock ashes at his ease. There are doors, up right, leading to the outer hallway, and down left, leading to the flower garden. To the right of the French doors is a telephone stand, with a telephone on it.*

AT THE RISE OF THE CURTAIN, DOT *is standing in the middle of the room, gazing furiously toward a pair of feet and a newspaper in the far right back corner, which are* DICK. *She is young, attractive in a spirited, impetuous, high tempered way. The owner of the feet turns another page and reads on.* DOT *stamps her foot furiously, then whirls, crosses and flounces into the chair down left.*

DOT: Dick, you make me absolutely sick! Do you hear it? Absolutely sick!

DICK: [*Has been arranging his paper, and he glances up long enough to say.*] Sorry, sis! [*He submerges once more.*]

DOT: [*Rising, and delivering her last and final "ultimatum".*] Then will you or will you not, meet the girls to-night, and act like a human being?

DICK: Will not.

DOT: Oh, darn! [*She flops, disconsolate, into her chair, and sits with her elbows on her knees.*] What in the name of sense is the use of having a famous brother if——

DICK: None.

DOT: Shut up!

DICK: Sure. Be glad to. You do the same. [*He tosses down his paper, rises, turns and picks up a cigarette from the stand and prepares to light it.*]

DOT: The last time I brought a lovely girl here to dinner, what did you do?

DICK: [*Glancing over his shoulder.*] Don't you know what I did?

DOT: Do I know? Well, I should rather say I do! When she asked you kindly, courteously, sweetly, just by way of making conversation——

DICK: [*Whirling about.*] Sweeeeeetly! Just by way of making conversation! Ye Gods, why are they always sweeeet, and why do they always have to make conversation?

DOT: Oh, shut up!

DICK: [*Beginning to be amused now, he moves down and sits on the arm of the divan, down stage.*] Sure. Shut up yourself. [*He prepares to smoke and enjoy the scrap.*]

DOT: [*She'd like to pull hair, but she has a point to make, so she muffles her desire to throttle him.*] She asked you why you always painted landscapes and animals, and never the human face, and what did you tell her? [*A silence—she stamps her foot.*] What did you tell her?

DICK: The truth.

DOT: [*Sinks, in blank despair, on the piano bench.*] The truth! My stars, haven't you learned any better than that, yet?

DICK: No.

DOT: You might at least have said something graceful or clever——

DICK: Graceful or clever! Oh, Lord!

DOT: And what did you say? What did you say?

DICK: [*With mock courtesy.*] I said, "The human face is already sufficiently painted, madame, and does not need any more paint!"

DOT: And made her perfectly furious!

DICK: Sure did! [*He strolls back, right, to grind out one cigarette and light another.*]

DOT: Dick, you didn't used to be like this. [*He wanders down, left, and sits on the arm of the easy chair there, gazing out into space.*] You used to be so nice and pleasant to all the girls. What's wrong?

DICK: [*Shortly, for she is treading on some ground—recently plowed, let us say.*] Nothing, sis.

DOT: Dick, you're not fooling me any! Who is she?

DICK: [*Impatiently, for she is getting entirely too close home.*] Who is who?

DOT: The girl! ! [*He gets up restlessly, and paces the floor, from left to right, and up and down,* Dot *always at his heels, aping his posture and his stride, through the next few lines.*]

DICK: There isn't any girl!

DOT: Is that so!

DICK: Yes, that's so!

DOT: It is not!

DICK: No?

DOT: Dick! Dick! [*He stops in the middle of the floor, and confronts her.*] I may be dumb and all that, but I know that no man is a woman hater without a reason. [*He retreats up right, to his haven of refuge, the cigarette stand.*]

DICK: Reasons for being a woman hater? There are always plenty of reasons. I understand there are to be at least a dozen reasons here tonight—playing bridge!

DOT: [*Mincingly.*] Who is she, Dick? Who told you once to—run along? Did she say never to speak to her again, Dick? Did she say——

DICK: For heaven's sake, shut up!

DOT: Dick, for the last time, are you or are you not, going to act like a civilized human being and meet the girls?

DICK: [*He walks deliberately to the center of the floor, and stands face to face, eye to eye, and almost nose to nose with her.*] I am not!

DOT: All right then, Dick! Look out! I gave you your chance! I am going to spread it around that you are a disappointed lover, and that that is why you are down on the women! And then, old boy, they'll just pester you to death! So there! [*Suddenly, and quite unaccountably, she flops down in the chair down left, and begins to cry.* DICK, *all contrition, hurries to her.*]

DICK: Why, child, don't cry! I didn't think it meant

anything to you! Why in creation do you want me to meet all those girls?

DOT: [*Wailing.*] *I* w-w-ant you to f-f-f-ind a girl you can be happy with—and—love——

DICK: Aw, honey! I'm happy enough! Right here with you!

DOT: But, you won't always have me.

DICK: [*Startled with the idea that after all she is no longer in pinafores, and chewing slate pencils.*] Dot! What do you mean? Are you and Harold—engaged?

DOT: [*Nods vigorously.*] And—and—you see I—I—I want you—I don't want you to be left all alone!

DICK: Dot! You getting married! Oh, I—see—why—why—well of—of course it's all right, and I'm happy for you, sis!

DOT: [*She flies to his arms, and searches in his coat pocket for a handkerchief with which she wipes her eyes.*] Oh, Dick, I'm so happy—but you'll be all alone! I'm so sad!

DICK: Oh, that's all right, little sis. [*He gazes out over her head, a little dazed.*]

DOT: [*Miraculously healed of her sorrow.*] Then Dick, won't you, just for me——

DICK: Oh, Lord, there you go again!

DOT: But, Dick, it wouldn't be hard to talk to them, would it?

DICK: [*Amused, he turns and crosses left, sitting on the lower arm of the divan.*] Hard work? Say, you don't have to talk to a woman! All you have to do is to get her where she can sit and rave to you about her secret yearnings! Secret yearnings! Blah!

DOT: Maybe you're right, Dick.

DICK: Maybe I'm right? I know darn well I'm right! Why, I'll bet you I could talk to every darn woman in that bridge club, and carry on a howlingly successful conversation, on two words!

DOT: On two words! Oh, come on now, Dick!

DICK: On two words!

DOT: What in the world would you say?

DICK: It wouldn't matter what I said. Something inane enough. The less meaning the better. How about——"Thanks awfully"?

DOT: Thanks awfully? A whole evening? Nothing else?

DICK: Absolutely!

DOT: [*Laughing,* DOT *crosses left to the console table and mirror, and fusses with her hair.*] Well, if you can get away with that, you're brighter than I thought you were!

DICK: [*Bowing elaborately.*] Thanks awfully!

DOT: [*Unconscious of what he has said.*] Oh, keep the change!

DICK: [*Even more elaborately.*] Thanks awfully.

DOT: Say, it does work, doesn't it? You old precious! [*Telephone rings.*]

DICK: [*Bowing again as* DOT *goes up center, to the telephone on a little stand beside the French doors.*] Thanks awfully.

DOT: [*At telephone.*] Hello—yes, this is Dot. A guest—sure, bring her right along! . . . Oh, that won't matter, there's nearly always an odd number anyway! . . . Sure—oh, Ann, who———I guess she's hung up. I was going to ask her who her guest is. I've heard the girls raving about her. [*Doorbell off right.*] Gee, there's some of them now. I'll bring them in and you can entertain them. [*Stopping in the door way up right, she turns with a grin.*] You sure can, all right! [*Exits.*]

DICK: [*At the mirror down, left, grooming himself for the slaughter.*] Thanks awfully!

DOT: [*Entering with* CAROL BARTON, *a brusque, mannish, athletic type of girl, rather man to man, and all that, and* EDITH CRANE, *fearfully self-conscious, with a little giggle, born to talk, and fulfilling her mission.*] Dick! [*He meets them center stage as she talks, and then with an elaborate grace, he bows over their hands, speaking first to* CAROL, *who stands at* DOT's *left, and then to* EDITH, *who is to her right.*] Here are two of my friends I've been wanting you to meet for a long time! Carol Jansen, and Edith Crane. [*As* DICK *bows over* EDITH's *hand, she crosses quickly in front of him, and turns him away from* CAROL *and* DOT.]

EDITH: Oh, Mr. Montague! You don't know how we've wanted to meet you! [DOT *and* CAROL, *with significant glances at each other, cross left and sit on the bench at the piano, where they take in the conversation with much evident amusement.*] I always said I was just dying to meet a real celebrity, and yet I knew very well that when I got a chance, I'd be too fussed to say a word, and I am now, absolutely fussed to pieces!

CAROL: Oh, you don't say now, Edith?

EDITH: [*Turning slowly left, she rewards* CAROL *with a freezing stare, which changes to a saccharine-sweet smile as she turns back to* DICK.] Isn't that just the way of it? I'm fussed to death now! Absolutely fussed to death! I declare I couldn't talk if I had to!

CAROL: Is that so? [*Again the smile and the freezing stare, and back again to the smile.*]

EDITH: You can understand how it is, don't you? Oh, I just knew you'd understand!

DICK: Thanks, awfully.

EDITH: Geniuses always understand so much more than mere mortals! [DICK *makes a deprecating gesture.*] Oh, you needn't try to deny it. He is a genius, isn't he, girls?

CAROL: [*Coming over to them, and shaking* DICK's *hand. When she approaches,* EDITH *shifts to the other side, to be ready to turn him away from* CAROL *again.*] Absolutely! From the ground up. The whole world is giving you the hand clap now, Mr. Montague!

DICK: Thanks, awfully.

CAROL: And why shouldn't they! The way you handled animals in that last study!

EDITH: [*With her hand on his arm, turning him away from* CAROL *again.*] Really, it was the most amazing thing I ever saw! I was absolutely fussed to pieces! I couldn't say a word! Not a word!

CAROL: Imagine it! Not a word!

EDITH: Oh, Mr. Montague——

DOT: Girls, you'll excuse me a few moments won't you? Those last minute things, you know——

CAROL: Sure, run right along!

DOT: And if any of the girls come——

EDITH: [*Crossing and seating herself in the chair down left as she speaks.*] Dear, you just run right along, and we'll entertain your brother for you till you get back.

DOT: [*Pauses in the French doors, center back, and winking at* DICK, *she speaks.*] Thanks, awfully! [*Exits.*]

EDITH: Now, Mr. Montague, let's sit down and talk, for I do want to ask you about some of your pictures! [DICK *and* CAROL *sit on the piano bench.*] You know, I've just studied and studied them, and——[*Doorbell.*] Oh, dear, there's the door bell! Carol, won't you answer it? And, tell them to take their coats off before they come in, because I want to talk to Mr. Montague before any of them——

CAROL: [*Amused, she turns in the doorway, up right, and calls.*] Talk right on, dear. I'll hold the mad mob at bay as long as I can. [*Exits.*]

DICK: [*To* CAROL, *as he sits again.*] Thanks awfully.

EDITH: What was I saying? Oh, yes, about the pictures: I want you to tell me all about them! You know the one that—that the one—well, anyway, when I look at them I just get the strangest feeling—like I was—answering something in them! You know, I just feel like I'd known the man who does them, for a long, long time!

DICK: Thanks, awfully.

EDITH: Oh, you're *so* understanding! I just know if I could ask you and have you explain everything, it would all be clear! [CAROL *enters with* MRS. DODD, *a martial, bossy soul, a regular manager of other people's affairs, and* MRS. SMYTHE, *who is fearfully cultuahed. One must cut the "R's" to suit.*] Oh bother, there they come! I wanted to talk to you a long, long time, but perhaps after a while——[*She crosses to them, sweetly smiling.*] Oh, how do you do, Mrs. Dodd, and Mrs. Smythe! [*She speaks last to* MRS. SMYTHE, *and the two of them move a little to the right, and stand by the table behind the divan, talking together.*]

CAROL: Mrs. Dodd, may I present Dot's brother? I'm sure you have heard of him!

MRS. DODD: [*She moves majestically toward* DICK, *as a ship in full sail.*] Ah, my dear young man! I have been wanting to talk to you for a long, long time!

DICK: Thanks, awfully!

MRS. DODD: For such a clever, talented boy, you are entirely too quiet and retiring! You ought to play up to your genius more! It deserves it!

DICK: Thanks, awfully!

MRS. DODD: You really ought. I am going to—but pardon me—Mrs. Smythe! [*She ushers him with a grand gesture, in upon the presence of* MRS. SMYTHE.] May I present Mr. Montague. One of our coming artists. In fact, I may safely say—one of our artists! For he is not merely coming—he has arrived.

DICK: Thanks, awfully!

MRS. SMYTHE: [*Drapes her finger tips in mid air, about the height of her eyes.*] Oh, Mr. Montague! I have been so interested in you, rehlly!

DICK: [*Taking on a touch of her boredom.*] Thanks, o-fully!

MRS. SMYTHE: You see, I hahve known youah fahmily. Quite intimately, I may say, and it is so delightful to see the scion of an old family coming to the foah in the world of aht!

DICK: Thanks, awfully!

[*Doorbell, and* CAROL *and* EDITH *go to answer it.*]

MRS. DODD: Mrs. Smythe, when the girls come back, don't you wish to start a table of bridge? I have some plans to talk over with Mr. Montague.

MRS. SMYTHE: Yes, it would, ah—be very well! [*She floats into the room, center back, and is seen cutting and making a deck of cards.*]

MRS. DODD: As I was saying, Mr. Montague, I want to give a large thé dansant in your honor, and give all the good people a chance to know you, to hear you talk. [DICK *stands in the center of the floor, wiping his forehead. He wishes he were dead.*]

DICK: Thanks, awfully.

MRS. DODD: [*She is wound up now, and ready to elocute.* CAROL *and* EDITH *enter with* ENID HOUSTEN, *all gush, and* NANETTE CARRINGTON, *tall, willowy, all lines, and undulating lines at that.* MRS. DODD *raves right on.*] Really, you artists owe it to us common folks to tell us all about your art! How else can we learn! In other words, the world is listening for you to speak!——Ah, my dear girls, Mrs. Smythe is waiting for some of you to play with her. [DICK *has moved up stage a little,* MRS. DODD *is seated with the air of a permanent fixture in the chair down left, and* NANETTE *moves down to the fireplace, down right, and drapes herself there.*]

ENID: Oh, Mrs. Dodd, we will just be thrilled to play, but we must speak to Dorothy's brother first. [*She moves toward him, all eyes and smiles.*]

CAROL: [*Crosses to center with* ENID.] Mr. Montague, I want you to meet Miss Enid Housten.

ENID: Oh, Mr. Montague, how perfectly thrilling! I never, never, never hoped to be so marvelously fortunate! Whatever possessed you to be so good to us, and to meet us tonight? I think it was perfectly precious of you!

DICK: Thanks, awfully!

ENID: Really, Mr. Montague, you are just too devastating for words! It is positively marvelous to look at those pictures of yours! Really it is!

DICK: Thanks, awfully!

MRS. DODD: [*Impatiently awaiting her turn again.*] I am sure Mrs. Smythe is ready for a hand of bridge now. Don't some of you girls want to play?

EDITH: [*Retreats to the chair up right.*] Really, I was talking to Mr. Montague, and I hadn't quite finished what I was saying.

CAROL: I'm awfully sorry, Mrs. Dodd, but I am answering the doorbell for Dot.

MRS. DODD: My dear girl, don't let that deter you! I shall be only too glad to relieve you of the task. Go right along. You younger ones enjoy your bridge, I know!

MRS. SMYTHE: [*Appearing in the doors, center back.*] Mrs. Dodd, I am counting on you for my partner. And Carol, won't you and Edith join us?

EDITH: Really, Mrs. Smythe, I am just wild to play, but I was talking to Mr. Montague—about—a——

ENID: Oh, my goodness gracious, let's leave Carol to answer the door, and all play! [*She attempts to drag* DICK *skillfully along with them, but it doesn't work.* MRS. DODD, MRS. SMYTHE, EDITH *and* ENID *go into the bridge room as* CAROL *speaks.*]

CAROL: Fine enough. Oh, Mr. Montague, you haven't met Miss Carrington yet. Nanette!—Nanette! [*The statue comes slowly to life.*]

NANETTE: Yes?

CAROL: Nanette, may I present Mr. Richard Montague, Dot's brother, Miss Carrington.

NANETTE: [*Undulating in his direction.*] Mr. Montague, this is—[*Much rolling of eyes.*]—charming—a moment to—long remember!

DICK: Thanks, awfully. [*Doorbell rings.*]

CAROL: Pardon me one moment. [*Exits up right.*]

NANETTE: [*Quite oblivious to all save the two of them—she is rather good at that—goes nearer* DICK *as he stands about center stage, and gazes at him soulfully.*] I cannot say how long I have been wishing—wishing in vain it seemed, that I might look into the eyes of the one who painted that marvelous "At Sunset" of yours. [*She is fairly draped against* DICK *by now. He moves away the merest fraction as he speaks.*]

DICK: Thanks, awfully.

NANETTE: [*Closer again, as* DICK *retreats. Through these next speeches he keeps edging imperceptibly further and further, and she draws closer and closer.*] You know, there is a warmth—a fire—a passion about your pictures that grips the very soul! The moment I saw your landscape I paused—I was held! There—I said—is the work of a man, a true man, a man who feels! [DOT *and* ENID *enter, coming down left.*]

DICK: [*Still retreating.*] Thanks awfully.

DOT: Is Dick meeting everyone?

ENID: [*To the right of* DOT, *gazing soulfully over at* DICK.] Oh, everybody! And we're positively fascinated with him! I mean, you know, he's too marvelous for words! Outrageously fascinating, really!

DOT: [*Catching* DICK's *eye, and knowing he can't wreak his vengeance on her.*] That's just fine! Dick has been so perfectly crazy to meet you girls. You must be awfully nice to him, and see just lots of him!

DICK: [*With looks that promise much for* DOT—*later.*] Thanks awfully!

NANETTE: [*Endeavoring to recapture* DICK.] It has all been very, very wonderful, Mr. Montague. I wonder if you know sometimes, just how few there are—[MRS. DODD, *quite impatient, stands in the French doors back stage.*]—who really answer to the inner cry for beauty—life—love—who answer it as you do! [DOT *is thoroughly amused, and* ENID *is disgusted that* NANETTE *is stealing her fire.*]

DICK: Thanks awfully.

MRS. DODD: Enid, we are dealing again!

ENID: Oh, I was just coming! [*She turns once more to* DICK.] I—I do so hope to talk with you again, Mr. Montague! [*Gazing back, she trails slowly toward the door.*]

DICK: Thanks awfully.

ENID: [*With a new idea, and a new ray of hope, she hurries back to them.*] Perhaps you'd like to take my hand this time, Nanette? [*Just a little too sweetly and smoothly, without the slightest trace of making the remark pointed.*] Or do you want—another hand?

NANETTE: [*Relinquishing her clasp of* DICK'S *hand, she turns away haughtily, down right.*] I care little for bridge.

ENID: [*Fires her parting shot with the same sweetness, and then exits.*] Today?—Too bad!

DOT: [*Going right, to cover the slightly strained silence.*] Wonderful evening, isn't it, Nanette?

NANETTE: [*Soulful again.*] Wonderful!—Wonderful! [*Oblivious to* DOT, *she turns on* DICK *again.*] Have you ever seen it so— [DOT, *left out in the cold, casts an expressive glance heavenward, and crosses left, to the arm of the chair.*]—so—intensely thrilling, Mr. Montague? I feel somehow as though a fire burned in me to answer to the flame of red upon the trees. [MRS. DODD *enters center back, and moves down stage, intent upon wresting* DICK *from* NANETTE.] I am only waiting to see a last and perfect portraiture of fall—when you paint it!

DICK: Thanks, awfully!

MRS. DODD: My dear Miss Carrington, I know you are dying to play! No—no—not a word! Not a word! I won't accept thanks! [*Moves left and seats herself with an air of finality in the arm chair there.*] Just go right along! I told them you were to have my hand. Not a word! Not a word! I am glad to do it!

NANETTE: But really, Mrs. Dodd, Mr. Montague and I were——

MRS. DODD: That's all right, perfectly all right! He'll excuse you, I am sure! [DICK *bows his head, and* NANETTE, *seeing no help for it, flows toward the door, center back, and into the bridge room.* DICK *goes as far as the door with her, and stands there, as though he might be contemplating flight, even at the price of bridge.*] I have some matters of business to talk over with him—some publicity work, and he will be glad to excuse you for the moment, I am sure. [*When* NANETTE *has quite departed.*] Now, my dear young man, I want to talk very seriously with you. [CAROL *appears up right with* MRS. HEMINGWAY *and* MRS. JAMES-GOWER. DOT *crosses to speak with them, and* CAROL *enters the bridge room.*] As I was saying, I want to have a regular lecture tea for you, and a thé dansant besides, for I want you to talk yourself into the good graces of our people!

DICK: Thanks, awfully!

DOT: [*Crossing to center with* MRS. HEMINGWAY, *who* has a nice, motherly smile, and MRS. JAMES-GOWER, *who is neither kindly, nor motherly, but waspish of build, of feature, and of tongue.*] Mrs. Hemingway, I think you know my brother. [DICK *moves down stage to meet them.*]

MRS. HEMINGWAY: Well, well, Dick, this is lovely! I suppose you don't remember me, do you? But I surely remember you, since you were just so high!

DICK: Thanks, awfully!

DOT: And, Mrs. James-Gower, may I present my brother, Mr. Montague.

MRS. JAMES: [*Acidly.*] Oh, how do you do, Mr. Montague! I presume you are quite delighted to be here tonight! Men generally are—not!

DICK: [*Laughing in relief at this turn of things.*] Thanks awfully!

MRS. HEMINGWAY: Now, I don't believe Dick minds the girls a bit! I used to know him rather well when he was young, and I can't remember any symptoms of the woman hater in him.

MRS. DODD: [*Majestically.*] An artist must not hate the ladies, for it is on them that his favour, his popularity, his very bread depends! Men have very little use for artists!

DICK: Thanks, awfully!

MRS. JAMES: Bread or no bread, I believe if I were a red-blooded man, I'd go hungry before I'd be some woman's lap dog, or drink tea with a bunch of them!

DICK: Thanks, *awfully!*

MRS. JAMES: Though I must say that some of the artistic people I have seen certainly don't mind being lionized!

MRS. HEMINGWAY: [*Comfortably.*] Now, now, Lucy, you'll make Dick feel bad! Dick may paint, but he's no ladies' man, and I've known him ever since fishing pole days!

DICK: [*Gratefully.*] Thanks, awfully!

MRS. HEMINGWAY: Well, you might thank me because I didn't use to spank you when you drew pictures on my wall paper. I used to think, even then, that some-day I'd be saying, "Oh, shucks, I knew him when——[*Doorbell rings, and* DOT *turns, up right.*]

DOT: Pardon me one moment. [*Exit.*]

MRS. DODD: Ladies—[*Seating herself with an air of permanence in the chair down left.*] I am sure you'll pardon me if I tear Mr. Montague away from you. I have some publicity plans, some teas and affairs to talk over with him——

MRS. JAMES: Certainly, the artists need their religion! They couldn't get along without their—"Ladies Aid", could they? [*Enter,* DOT *up right, with* CAROLYN BARTON *and* JANE VAN SICKLE.]

MRS. DODD: [*Rising in majesty.*] Mr. Montague, perhaps if we went into the garden and talked a while, the ladies would excuse us.

DICK: [*Weakly.*] Thanks awfully.

DOT: Dick, I want you to meet Carolyn Barton. [MRS. DODD *waits impatiently by her chair, down left;* MRS. JAMES-GOWER *is down right by the divan;* DICK *and* MRS. HEMINGWAY *up left, and* DOT *and the two girls up right.* CAROLYN *runs with little, childish steps, to* DICK, *and proceeds to "thrill".*]

CAROLYN: Oh, Mithter Montague, I juth knew you were you the minute I thet eyeths on you! Coth I've theen tho many picthurths of you! Perfectly darling oneths, too! Weely!

DICK: Thanks, awfully!

CAROLYN: [*Taking him by the hands, she leads him back to* JANE, *center stage.*] And, oh Mithter Montague! Thith ith Mith Jane Van Thickle! Jane ith tho bwainy! The ith going to have a caweeah—and be famouth—juth like you!

DICK: Thanks, awfully!

JANE: [*Shaking hands with him.*] Mr. Montague, this is indeed a rare privilege.

DICK: Thanks, awfully!

JANE: It is a privilege I have looked forward to so very, very long. You really can't imagine how some of us who have not yet made our mark strive toward the goal——

MRS. DODD: My dear girls, I am sure you will excuse Mr. Montague a few moments, for we have some matters of great importance——

CAROLYN: [*Runs to her, pleadingly.*] Oh, Mithith Dodd, we have juth come!

MRS. JAMES: We're not responsible for the time we can begin playing. You know what time the club starts, or is supposed to start, I hope! [*Starts toward the door, center back.*] Come, Mrs. Hemingway, let us begin. [*Exit, the two.*]

CAROLYN: [*Gazing after the "dear departed", her finger in her mouth.*] Oh, Mithith Jameth-Gowah, how fwightfully cwooel you theem to be! Weely!

JANE: As I was saying, Mr. Montague, you cannot imagine how some of us who have not yet made our mark——

MRS. DODD: Mr. Montague, I am sure the ladies will excuse you——

JANE: [*Disappointed.*] Oh, yes indeed!

DICK: Thanks, awfully. [*He falters one moment, but is game, and goes as a lamb to the slaughter.* CAROLYN *who has skipped over to speak with* DOT *the moment before, now runs back, as though to follow* DICK, *and, climbing into the chair down left, she gazes after him with all the tragic sorrow of a lost kitten.*]

CAROLYN: Oh, I think itth juth fwightfully cwooel to take him away fwum uth, don't you, Dot?

DOT: [*Smiling.*] Fwightful!

JANE: [*Moving with much stateliness, toward the end of the divan and gazing soulfully into the ethereal distances—the fifth dimension, or the rarefied altitudes.*] I would have enjoyed so much asking him about so many things! Artists have so much in common!

CAROLYN: [*Innocently—too innocently, perhaps.*] Oh, Jane, itth a good thing Mithith Jameth-Gowah didn't heah you wefer to yourself ath an artitht, or the would thay thomething fwightfully cwooel—I juth know the would!

JANE: [*Wounded dignity, descending from Olympia.*] You mean to say you think I am not——

CAROLYN: [*With a pretty little gesture, her eyes wider than ever.*] Oh, goodneth, no! I wath juth thpeaking of Mithith Jameth-Gowah! [*Doorbell rings.*]

DOT: [*Going toward door up right.*] That must be Ann and her guest. She phoned to me that she had a guest who had just arrived, and that she was bringing her along. [*Exit.*]

CAROLYN: Oh, I'm juth fwilled to death! They thay her gueтht thudied in Pawith for theveral yearth, and I'm juth dying to thee her! I juth love people who have thtudied in Pawith! I think itth what maketh Mithter Montague tho thweet!

JANE: Oh, do you!

[DOT *enters with* ANN MARSH, *and* MARION GATEWOOD. CAROLYN *runs across to* ANN, *and gazes at* MARION.]

CAROLYN: But, you know thom timeth, I think it maketh them fwightfully cwooel, too! Weely I do! [*She crosses to* ANN.] Oh, Ann, I've juth been heawing thutch weely wonderful thingth about your guetht—weely I have!

ANN: I s'pect they're all true! Marion, I want you to know Carolyn Barton—and Jane Van Sickle—Marion Gatewood.

Carolyn *JANE:* They tell me you have had the rare privilege of studying in Paris. thudied in Pawith

DOT: Oh, how exciting!

MARION: [*Very charming, very much at ease.*] Yes, I spent four very lovely years there.

CAROLYN: Oh, I think it would be wonderful—juth wonderful weely! But you know, thom timeth I think that Pawith can make you fwightfully cwooel—weely I do!

MARION: [*Amused.*] You what? Think Paris can make you cruel? Well—it may be that you are right—[*Her mind is away off now.*] But sometimes Paris can be rather cruel, too!

DOT: My brother studied in Paris. And I think you're right about it. I know it changed Dick.

MARION: [*Merely politely interested.*] It did? As a general thing, Miss—pardon me, but I did not understand your name, when Ann introduced us. It is scandalous not to know my hostess, isn't it?

DOT: Montague—Dorothy Montague. I was wondering if——

MARION: [*Crossing right, toward the divan, and keeping her face turned from them.*] Montague? You say your brother——

DOT: Yes, Dick studied in Paris. He is a painter. And I wondered if by chance you——

MARION: Dick Montague!! Well I should rather say———[*A little pause, and she regains her control.*] Yes, I knew him—in Paris.

CAROLYN: [*Running left, and then stopping.*] Oh, how fwightfully fwilling! I juth mutht tell Mithter Montague! Where ith Mithter Montague?

JANE: Oh, Mrs. Dodd has him cornered, talking business in the moonlight!

MRS. SMYTHE: [*From the French doors.*] Carolyn! Jane! Ann! Shall we begin now? And where is Mrs. Dodd?

ANN: [*Much amused.*] We hear she's talking business in the moonlight, Mrs. Smythe. [CAROLYN *and* JANE *exit back center, with* MRS. SMYTHE.]

MARION: Miss Montague—Ann—I really can't stay!

ANN: Why, Marion, are you ill?

DOT: Miss Gatewood—what is it? I was so anxious for you to see Dick.

MARION: I—I—don't know how to try to explain it—but I knew Dick awfully well—well enough to—to—quarrel very bitterly—and I vowed I would never see him again, and I—I—just can't see him here tonight! I simply can't face it!

DOT: Oh, please don't go!

MARION: I'm sorry but I——

ANN: Quick! Into the other room, Marion! They're coming!

MARION: But I——

DOT: Play bridge—Dick won't come in there! [*She and* ANN *push* MARION *into the bridge room, and return, closing the doors.*] Now, where is he?

ANN: [*Laughing.*] Out in the garden, I guess!

DOT: Didn't you hear him coming?

ANN: [*Airily.*] No!

DOT: Then, why——

ANN: I just didn't want her to go home. Now, before Dick does come, let's scheme a little!

DOT: I'll bet anything that's the girl Dick loves! There certainly is someone!

ANN: That's what I've figured out, old dear. That's why she wasn't sure who you were—and I didn't tell you who she was, so you could spill the beans before Dick. Wonder what they'll say when they see each other?

DOT: [DOT *flops down on the divan with a squeal of delight.*] Oh my eye, Ann! There's only one thing Dick can say! Thanks awfully!

ANN: Thanks awfully?

DOT: That's all! We've got a bet on! That's all he's going to say the whole evening!

MARION: [*In the French doors.*] Ann! [*The girls start, and turn.*] I can go now. He didn't come in, did he?

MRS. DODD: [*Off stage, just without the door down left.*] My dear young man, I think these plans [*Enters, followed by* DICK.] will be the making of you.

DICK: Thanks, awfully. [*He sees* MARION, *and they*

both stand as though frozen. Then MARION *disappears.*]

ANN: I was waiting for you, Mrs. Dodd. Shall we play?

MRS. DODD: Yes—yes—and now, my dear Mr. Montague, if you think of anything else [*She moves toward the French doors with* ANN.] you wish to talk about, just interrupt at any time—any time. I shan't mind at all—not at all!

DICK: [*Mechanically, for he is standing motionless, staring toward the French doors.*] Thanks, awfully. [*Exit,* MRS. DODD *and* ANN.] Dot, who in the world was that girl?

DOT: [*Determined to have a little fun.*] Whoa, there, Dick! "Thanks awfully" is your conversation tonight!

DICK: Oh, Dot, for Heaven's sake, I——

DOT: How about it, Dick? It was a bargain!

DICK: Dot, I just can't let this chance go by to talk to her! I just have to explain! You don't know how much it means!

DOT: I promised her she wouldn't have to see you, Dick, and I can't break my promise—even if you are breaking yours!

DICK: Have a heart! I tell you, this is serious!

DOT: [*Thoroughly delighted and enjoying herself hugely.*] Tell you what Dick—if you'll keep your bargain about "Thanks awfully" I'll send her in here. How about it?

DICK: Look here, sis! [*He pulls out a chain on which hangs a diamond ring.*] Dot, when Marion wore that ring, I was the happiest man that ever lived. Aren't you going to give me a chance?

DOT: If you keep your bargain!

DICK: Do you expect a man to get engaged to a girl on two words?

DOT: Sure! All they ever say is "Will you?" and the girl says the rest! Maybe Marion is modern, and she'll propose, and then you can say, "Thanks, awfully!"

DICK: Oh, damn!

DOT: Oh, all right! But you had your chance! And you missed it! [*Starts toward door.*]

DICK: Dot, come back here!

DOT: Sorry, old man—nothing doing!

DICK: Dot, come here!

DOT: Sorry! Too late now!

DICK: Dot, I promise!

DOT: [*Turning.*] Absolutely? On your honor?

DICK: [*Through his teeth.*] Absolutely! On my honor!

DOT: Not a word but "Thanks awfully."

DICK: Absolutely.

DOT: You won't break your promise?

DICK: [*Grimly.*] I'll keep it if it kills me, damn it!

DOT: Good boy! [*Exits.*]

[*Left alone,* DICK *paces frantically, rubs his head, straightens his tie, finally pauses, down right center, and taking the ring from the chain, puts it on his little finger.* MARION *enters,—there is a little click of the doors closing, and* DICK *jumps, then stands rigid.*]

MARION: [*Very much in love, very determined to play fair, and still very proud.*] Dick, I didn't know when I came here—or I declare I wouldn't have come——

DICK: [*Grimly.*] Thanks awfully.

MARION: Oh, I didn't mean it to sound that way! I didn't mean that I didn't—didn't want to see you!

DICK: Thanks, awfully.

MARION: [*She starts to lose her temper; then she remembers that she was in the wrong, and she continues.*] I know you think I was a cad, Dick. I know now I was. I've regretted it often enough since then.

DICK: [*Gesturing futilely, then mutters.*] Thanks, awfully.

MARION: [*Puzzled, hurt, furious all in one. Then she continues.*] Dick! [*She comes down right, and stands quite close to him.*] Aren't you even going to look at me, Dick? Dick? Please—I—I—want you to, Dick!

DICK: [*Turns, his hands clenching and unclenching behind him.*] Thanks, awfully.

MARION: [*Whirling away from him.*] Oh, be as sarcastic as you wish! [DICK *reaches toward her, then stops, and flings out his hands in desperation.*] Dick, I have found out since that the things I believed of you were lies!

DICK: Thanks, awfully.

MARION: If it had been any ordinary lover's quarrel—but I feel it was something worth trying to save—even at this price———

DICK: [*Almost beside himself. His words are barely audible.*] Thanks, awfully.

MARION: [*Staring straight ahead, wistfully.*] Dick, when I was little, I prided myself on being a white sport—and when I was wrong I admitted it. I have been fighting that white sport in me every since that night we quarreled. Tonight, the white sport says—I'm sorry, Dick! [*She comes quite close to him, and makes a little, tender gesture over his shoulder, almost touching it. Then, giving up, she turns away.*] I—I—guess that's all. [DICK *opens his mouth to speak, realizes it is useless, makes a head long dive toward her, and catches her in his arms. She clings to him, sobbing. He endeavors to comfort her with desperate little pattings. The door center back opens, admitting* DOT, *who strolls in quite casually, and gazes at the oblivious pair.*]

DOT: Oh, I was just going! [*Exits, closing the door.*]

DICK: [*Meaning it.*] Thanks, awfully!!!!

MARION: Dick—I—I—don't know why I'm crying—just because I'm happy! [*He puts the ring on her finger.*] Oh, Dick, you kept it all this time! You old precious! [*She gives him a little, swift, ecstatic kiss.*]

DICK: [*Holds her off for a moment, smiling down into her eyes.*] Thanks, AWFULLY!!!

CURTAIN